MW00900245

This book

belongs

to Emily

If found

Pelse

Bring

to me!

Uniflower